LOVENDA MCHAYLE-JACK

SPIRITUALITY MADE SIMPLE

A guidebook crafted to accompany you on your profound voyage of spiritual exploration and self-discovery.

ABOUT THIS BOOK

"Spirituality Made Simple" is a comprehensive guidebook that explores spirituality in a modern context, focusing on personal growth and development. It delves into the essence of spirituality, debunking common myths and misconceptions while distinguishing between spirituality and organized religion. The book emphasizes the importance of personalizing one's spiritual journey, encouraging readers to explore their inner selves and beliefs to discover their unique path.

HOW IT CAN HELP YOU

Personal Growth and Development: The book provides practical insights and tools to facilitate personal growth and development, helping readers cultivate a deeper understanding of themselves and their place in the world. By debunking myths surrounding spirituality, the book clears away misconceptions that may hinder personal growth. It offers clarity and guidance for those navigating their spiritual journey in a world filled with conflicting information.

Differentiating Religion and Spirituality: Understanding this is crucial for individuals seeking a more personalized approach to their spiritual journey. "Spirituality Made Simple" encourages the exploration of this difference, empowering readers to forge their own spiritual path regardless of religious affiliations.

Personalizing Spiritual Journey: Recognizing that spirituality is a deeply personal experience, the book encourages readers to tailor their journey to their own beliefs, values, and experiences. It provides guidance on how to tap into one's inner wisdom and intuition to create a meaningful spiritual practice.

Suggested Activities: Throughout the book, readers will find practical exercises and activities designed to deepen their spiritual exploration. These activities range from mindfulness practices and journaling prompts to rituals and meditations, offering a hands-on approach to spiritual growth.

Overall, **"Spirituality Made Simple"** serves as a supportive companion for anyone embarking on or seeking to deepen their spiritual journey. It offers a blend of philosophical insights, practical guidance, and experimental activities aimed at fostering personal transformation and inner fulfillment.

LOVENDA MCHAYLE-JACK
FOUNDER OF SPIRITUAL ESSENTIALS

Lovenda McHayle-Jack owner and creator of Spiritual Essentials, LLC, and a dedicated spiritual life coach and Alchemist.

With a deep-rooted connection to my faith as a child of the Most High God, my life revolves around my roles as a mother to seven incredible children and a devoted wife to my first love. Beyond these titles, I cherish the roles as a daughter, sister, aunt, cousin, niece, and friend, all of which have shaped me into the person I am today. These roles serve as pillars of humility and grounding, guiding me through life's journey with pride and authenticity. Blessed with extraordinary spiritual gifts and abilities since the age of two, I possess the unique ability to communicate with spirits, perceive events across time, and intuitively sense the experiences of others.

Through my unwavering faith in God and with the guidance of my spiritual team of ancestors and spirit guides, I have honed my gifts through prayer, fasting, and spiritual practices. These gifts have enabled me to assist myself, family, and others in profound ways, often leaving me in awe of the spiritual experiences and encounters. Motivated by a desire to share my knowledge and guide others on their spiritual journey.

I have authored this instructional book Drawing from my personal experiences, spiritual insights, and practical wisdom, this book offers readers a roadmap for navigating their own spiritual paths with clarity, authenticity, and empowerment. Through her writing, I seek to inspire others to embrace their spiritual gifts, connect with their inner selves, and experience the transformative power of spirituality in their lives.

PREFACE

Welcome to "**Spirituality Made Simple**," a straightforward and informative guide designed to support you on your spiritual journey. This book is formatted as a collection of frequently asked questions (FAQs) about spirituality, covering topics such as God, the Bible, faith, energy, spiritual tools and tokens, and how to effectively use them for healing, protection, and prosperity.

The aim of "**Spirituality Made Simple**" is to provide readers with practical insights and guidance to deepen their understanding of themselves and their spiritual path. By developing and nurturing a relationship with God, ancestors, and spirit guides, readers will learn how to harness their unique gifts and abilities for personal growth and transformation. Throughout this book, you'll discover the importance of establishing and maintaining healthy boundaries to strengthen your spiritual practice.

You'll also learn how to trust yourself as you navigate the journey of enhancing your intuition and discernment.

As you embark on this journey, I encourage you to approach the material with an open mind and a willingness to explore new perspectives. If this book proves helpful to you, I kindly ask that you share it with others who may benefit from its insights.

Thank you in advance for your openness and willingness to embark on this journey of spiritual growth and discovery.

Warm regards,

CONTENTS

1
MYTHS ABOUT SPIRITUALITY

2
PERSONALIZING YOUR SPIRITUALITY

3
MEDITATION & TECHNIQUES

4
FREQUENCY OF MEDITATION

5
UNDERSTANDING DUALITY AND THE SHADOW

CONTENTS

6
UNDERSTANDING FEAR IN SPIRITUALITY (Q&A)

7
UNDERSTANDING SPIRITUAL HYGIENE

8
HONORING YOUR ANCESTORS

9
MANIFESTATION

10
TOOLS AND TOKENS

CONTENTS

11
UNDERSTANDING CHAKRAS

12
CALENDAR CYCLES

13
ELEMENTAL ENERGY

14
CAREFUL CONSUMPTION

MYTHS ABOUT SPIRITUALITY

CHAPTER 1
MYTHS ABOUT SPIRITUALITY

In our modern society, spirituality often carries a veil of mystery and misconception, leading some individuals to shy away from exploring their spiritual selves. However, it's essential to dispel these myths and misconceptions to encourage a deeper understanding and appreciation of spirituality.

Let's address some of the common myths that may deter people from embracing spirituality:

Myth: Spirituality is for Atheists or Non-believers.
Actually: Contrary to popular belief, spirituality often involves profound belief in a divine being or higher power. Many spiritual practitioners find that their faith in God or a higher powerstrengthens their spiritual journey. As stated in John 4:24, "God is a Spirit: and they that worship him must worship him in spirit and in truth."

It's important to recognize that spiritual beliefs, practices, and faith are deeply personal and subjective aspects of human experiences. Therefore, the idea of "converting" someone's spiritual beliefs or faith can be problematic because it assumes that there is a superior or correct belief system that everyone should adhere to. Instead of focusing on conversion, it's more constructive to foster an environment of mutual respect, understanding, and tolerance for diverse spiritual beliefs and practices.

Encouraging open dialogue, empathy, and acceptance allows individuals to share their perspectives without fear of judgment or pressure to conform. Spiritual growth and fulfillment are not necessarily tied to specific beliefs or practices. People can find meaning, purpose, and connection to something greater than themselves through a wide variety of spiritual paths. Respecting each person's journey allows for greater diversity and richness within the human experience of spirituality.

Myth: Spirituality is Cult-like.

Actually: While spirituality emphasizes individuality, it also fosters community and connection. Gathering with like-minded individuals to share beliefs and experiences can be enriching and supportive. As mentioned in Matthew 18:20, "For where two or three are gathered together in my name, am I in the midst of them."

Much like church or any other religious gathering spiritual communities can offer acceptance, encouragement, and inspiration to explore new ideas and experiences. They may gather for rituals, ceremonies, meditation sessions, or other shared practices that help foster spiritual growth and connections. Additionally, the community can serve as a source of guidance and wisdom, as members share their insights and experiences. Ultimately, a spiritual community can offer companionship and camaraderie on the path of spiritual exploration, providing a sense of connection that nourishes the soul.

Myth: Spirituality is Associated with Voodoo or Witchcraft.

Actually: Voodoo and witchcraft are specific spiritual practices among many, and they do not define spirituality as a whole. Spirituality encompasses a broad spectrum of beliefs and practices, and it's important not to conflate it with specific cultural or religious practices.

Spirituality encompasses a wide range of beliefs, experiences, and practices that vary greatly from person to person and from culture to culture. It can include aspects such as connection to nature, personal growth, meditation, prayer, and the search for meaning and purpose in life. By recognizing the diversity of spiritual experiences and beliefs, we can appreciate the richness of spirituality and the many paths that individuals may take on their spiritual journey. No single tradition or practice can fully define spirituality, as it is ultimately a deeply personal and subjective aspect of human existence.

Myth: One must be initiated into or be a devotee of a specific spiritual or religious organization to be considered spiritual.

Actually: Being spirituality is a personal journey, and one's connection to higher aspects of existence can be cultivated through various paths, not necessarily tied to organized religion or specific practices. Many people find connection and enlightenment through introspection, mindfulness, nature, creativity, or simply by being present in the moment. It's about tapping into the essence of who you are and the interconnectedness of all things. Spirituality is about connecting with the deeper aspects of oneself, seeking meaning, purpose, and connection to something greater. This journey can take many forms and is unique to each individual. While some may find guidance and support within organized religious or spiritual communities, others may find their spiritual path through personal exploration, introspection, or connection with nature.

My spiritual initiations or elevation happened through the guidance of the Holy Spirit and my spiritual team is more valid and meaningful to me than any organized initiation ritual could have provided.

Many people have deeply personal and profound spiritual experiences outside of organized formal rituals. The Holy Spirit, often understood as the divine presence of God within individuals, can work in mysterious and unexpected ways to lead people on their spiritual journey.

These intimate experiences of spiritual connection and guidance are valuable and can be transformative, shaping one's understanding of themselves, their purpose, and their relationship to the divine.

Regardless of whether they occur within the context of a religious or spiritual organization or through individual exploration, such experiences can be significant in one's spiritual development. Ultimately, spirituality is about the relationship between the individual and the divine, however, they may conceive it, and it is not limited by adherence to any particular organization or tradition.

Myth: Hierarchy in spirituality.

Actually: This common spiritual myth about hierarchy is the belief that one must ascend through various levels or stages to reach enlightenment or spiritual fulfillment.

This idea can create a sense of competition or inadequacy among practitioners, leading to feelings of superiority or inferiority based on perceived spiritual attainment. In reality, spiritual growth is a personal journey, and there is no one-size-fits-all path to enlightenment. Each individual's journey is unique, and spiritual progress cannot be accurately measured or compared. It's important to remember that all beings are inherently worthy and capable of accessing their higher selves and divine connection, regardless of where they may perceive themselves within any hierarchical structure.

"For promotion cometh neither from the east, nor from the west, Nor from the south. But God is the judge: He putteth down one, and setteth up another."Psalm 75:6-7

Myth: Spiritual gifts are demonic.

This myth about spiritual gifts is the misconception that any form of supernatural ability or intuition is inherently demonic or evil. This belief often stems from religious teachings that associate such phenomena with negative forces or entities. However, many spiritual traditions and belief systems view these gifts as natural aspects of human consciousness or divine blessings.

Actually: In reality, spiritual gifts can include a wide range of abilities, such as intuition, empathy, healing, and mediumship, among others. These gifts are often seen as tools for personal growth, healing, and helping others, rather than being inherently harmful or demonic. It's essential to approach these gifts with discernment and ethical responsibility, but demonizing them based on fear or misunderstanding can hinder one's spiritual development and potential for positive impact in the world.

Myth: Spiritual gifts are demonic.

This myth about spiritual gifts is the misconception that any form of supernatural ability or intuition is inherently demonic or evil. This belief often stems from religious teachings that associate such phenomena with negative forces or entities. However, many spiritual traditions and belief systems view these gifts as natural aspects of human consciousness or divine blessings.

Actually: In reality, spiritual gifts can include a wide range of abilities, such as intuition, empathy, healing, and mediumship, among others. These gifts are often seen as tools for personal growth, healing, and helping others, rather than being inherently harmful or demonic. It's essential to approach these gifts with discernment and ethical responsibility, but demonizing them based on fear or misunderstanding can hinder one's spiritual development and potential for a positive impact in the world.

Myth: The Bible's condemnation of spirituality.

This myth about the Bible is the misconception that it universally condemns all forms of spiritual practices outside of its teachings. While the Bible does contain passages cautioning against certain practices, such as divination or witchcraft, it's essential to understand the historical and cultural context in which these prohibitions were written. Some interpretations of these passages have led to the belief that all non-religious spiritual practices are inherently sinful or condemned. However, this perspective ignores the diversity of spiritual beliefs and practices found throughout human history and across different cultures.

Actually: In reality, the Bible itself contains examples of various spiritual experiences, such as prophecy, visions, and encounters with angels. Moreover, many modern religious scholars interpret these passages as cautionary against practices that may lead to idolatry, exploitation, or harm, rather than a blanket condemnation of all spiritual exploration.

Ultimately, interpretations of the Bible's teachings on spirituality vary widely among different religious traditions and individuals, and it's essential to approach these texts with nuance and critical thinking.

Myth: Crystals are Evil Tools.

Actually: The notion that crystals are inherently evil is unfounded. Crystals have been mentioned throughout the Bible as precious stones and have been used in various contexts, including the breastplate of righteousness worn by the high priest Aaron (Exodus 28:15-21). Crystals can be utilized for healing, protection, and spiritual growth, in alignment with one's beliefs and intentions.

It's crucial to approach spirituality with an open mind and a willingness to explore its multifaceted nature. Reading the Bible or other religious and spiritual texts as well as engaging in personal reflection can be a valuable resource on your spiritual journey, allowing you to discern truth from myth and deepen your connection with the divine.

One effective way to address myths and misconceptions is through education and dialogue. Encouraging respectful conversations and sharing diverse viewpoints can help dispel misunderstandings and foster greater understanding and acceptance. Additionally, personal experience and introspection play a crucial role in navigating spiritual beliefs and practices.

By exploring our own beliefs and experiences, we can gain insight into what resonates with us individually and discern what feels authentic and meaningful. Ultimately, embracing complexity and uncertainty while remaining open to new ideas can lead to a deeper and more enriching spiritual journey. As we continue to explore and learn, we can challenge myths and misconceptions and cultivate a more inclusive and compassionate understanding of spirituality.

Chapter Guidance: By addressing these myths and misconceptions through research, education, and personal exploration, individuals can overcome barriers and embark on a fulfilling spiritual journey that aligns with their beliefs and values.

CHAPTER QUESTION
What are some myths or misconceptions that may be prohibiting you from embracing your spiritual journey?

PERSONALIZING YOUR SPIRITUALITY

CHAPTER 2
PERSONALIZING YOUR SPIRITUALITY

Just as every individual is unique, so is their spiritual journey. Our understanding, practices, abilities, and gifts in spirituality vary greatly among individuals. While some may share similar abilities, each person's beliefs and practices are shaped by their experiences and perspectives.

However, within the spiritual community, there exists a division between those who seek to use spirituality for positive purposes such as peace, healing, protection, and prosperity, and those who misuse it for darker intentions. Spirituality, at its core, should serve as a guiding force to keep us grounded and connected to the divine – whether it be God, our ancestors, or the universe. It is a means to pass on wisdom, expand traditional customs, and deepen our knowledge of the spiritual realm.

Unfortunately, some individuals abuse their spiritual abilities, channeling negative energy to cause harm and discord in both the spiritual and physical realms. Their intentions often aim to derail others from their true calling or purpose. To navigate your spiritual journey effectively, it is crucial to understand your abilities and how to use them ethically. Without proper guidance and information, it is easy to become lost or misguided, leading to the misuse of spiritual gifts. Self-discovery is an ongoing process, requiring introspection and understanding of your strengths and areas for improvement.

Self-awareness is pivotal in protecting oneself from manipulation and exploitation by others, particularly within spiritual or faith-based contexts. Some practitioners and religious groups prey on individuals' lack of knowledge, understanding, and desperation, using their vulnerabilities to siphon energy for negative purposes.

By knowing yourself fully and understanding the intricacies of self-discovery, you can safeguard against such exploitation and maintain integrity in your spiritual practice. By embracing self-awareness and personalized spirituality, individuals can empower themselves to harness their abilities for positive transformation and growth.

Through continuous self-discovery and ethical practice, one can navigate their spiritual journey with clarity, purpose, and integrity. Remember, your spirituality is uniquely yours – honor it, nurture it, and let it guide you toward fulfillment and enlightenment. To personalize your spirituality, setting intentions and establishing boundaries are fundamental steps in aligning your spiritual practice with your goals and values.

HERE ARE SOME CONSIDERATIONS
TO GUIDE YOU IN THIS PROCESS:
Starting Your Journey

Clarify Your Intentions
Reflect on why you are pursuing spirituality and what you hope to achieve through your practice. Setting clear intentions can help you stay focused and aligned with your goals.

Identify Your Values
Consider what principles and beliefs are important to you. Integrating these values into your spiritual practice can provide a sense of purpose and direction.

Establish Boundaries
Determine what behaviors, practices, and energies are acceptable to you and what crosses the line. Setting boundaries is essential for maintaining your well-being and integrity on your spiritual journey.

Explore Different Practices
Be open to exploring various spiritual practices and traditions to find what resonates with you. Personalizing your spirituality may involve incorporating elements from different traditions or creating your own rituals.

Practice Self-Reflection
Regularly take time to reflect on your spiritual experiences, insights, and growth. Self-reflection can deepen your understanding of yourself and your spirituality.

Stay Open-Minded
Remain open to new ideas, perspectives, and experiences. Personalized spirituality is a dynamic and evolving process, and being open-minded allows for continued growth and exploration.

Listen to Your Inner Guidance
Trust your intuition and inner wisdom to guide you in making decisions and navigating your spiritual path. Pay attention to signs, synchronicities, and gut feelings.

Embrace Self-Expression
Express your spirituality in ways that feel authentic and meaningful to you. Whether through art, music, writing, or other creative outlets, allow your unique self to shine through.

Practice Gratitude
Cultivate gratitude for the blessings and lessons in your life, both spiritual and mundane. Gratitude can deepen your connection to the divine and foster a sense of abundance and contentment.

Chapter Guidance: By setting clear intentions and establishing boundaries, you empower yourself to navigate your spiritual journey with purpose, clarity, and integrity. Stay connected to your intentions, remain mindful of your boundaries, and trust in the guidance of the divine as you work towards manifesting your goals and fulfilling your spiritual purpose.

my journal

MEDITATION & TECHNIQUES

CHAPTER 3
MEDITATION & TECHNIQUES

Meditation is a powerful practice that cultivates mindfulness, and inner peace.

The Purpose of Meditation

Meditation serves to cultivate a sense of calm, peace, and balance, enhancing overall health and well-being. It provides a means to cope with the stresses of daily life by redirecting attention to calming influences. Through meditation, individuals can learn to stay centered and maintain inner peace amidst life's challenges. Here are some effective meditation techniques:

1. Focused Attention Meditation:
This form of meditation involves directing focused attention to a specific object or anchor, such as the breath. The objective is to maintain awareness and concentrate on the chosen focal point, allowing thoughts to come and go without attachment.
To practice focused attention meditation:
Find a comfortable seated position and close your eyes.
Begin to focus your attention on your breath, noticing the sensations of each inhale and exhale.
If your mind starts to wander, gently guide your attention back to the breath without judgment or frustration.
Continue this practice for a predetermined amount of time, gradually increasing the duration as you become more comfortable with the practice.
Body scan meditation is a wonderful practice for promoting relaxation and mindfulness. By systematically bringing awareness to each part of the body, you can release tension and cultivate a deeper connection between your mind and body. Remember to breathe deeply and consciously release any tension you encounter. Over time, this practice can lead to increased relaxation, stress reduction, and overall well-being.

2. Visualization meditation is a powerful technique that harnesses the mind's ability to create and manipulate mental images. Here are some examples of visualization meditation:

Visualization for Observation and Change:
In this form of visualization meditation, you are invited to picture places, people, and situations in your mind. The focus shifts from the breath to a mental image, allowing you to observe the mind and focus on physical sensations and insights.

To practice visualization for observation and change:
Find a comfortable seated position and close your eyes.
Begin by visualizing a specific place, person, or situation in your mind's eye. It could be a memory, a desired outcome, or a scene from nature.
Notice any physical sensations, emotions, or thoughts that arise as you visualize the image. Take note of any insights or areas for personal growth that come to mind.
Use the visualization as an opportunity to reflect on things, people, or situations you may need to change to improve your overall well-being.
Continue to observe and explore the visualization, allowing yourself to immerse fully in the experience while maintaining awareness of your breath and body surroundings.

my journal

FREQUENCY OF MEDITATION

CHAPTER 4
FREQUENCY OF MEDITATION

Daily meditation practice is recommended, even if only for a few minutes each day. Consistency is key in establishing and reinforcing the benefits of meditation, fostering a deeper connection with oneself and the environment.

Benefits of Meditation
Regular meditation practice leads to increasedgrounding, self-connection, and harmony within oneself
and with others. It promotes a sense of peace and calmness across the mind, body, and spirit, facilitating overall well-being.

Chapter Guidance: Meditation, yoga, and body scan exercise is utilized to bring awareness to one's spiritual, mental, emotional, and physical states. By systematically focusing on different parts of the mind and body, individuals can refocus on a state of oneness.

Create a daily meditation schedule.

UNDERSTANDING DUALITY AND THE SHADOW

CHAPTER 5
UNDERSTANDING DUALITY AND THE SHADOW

Understanding duality and the shadow involves recognizing and accepting the opposing aspects within ourselves. Duality refers to the coexistence of contrasting forces or qualities, such as good and evil, light and dark. The shadow, a concept from Jungian psychology, represents the unconscious parts of our personality that we repress or deny. Exploring these aspects can lead to self-awareness, personal growth, and integration of our whole selves.

Duality is a fundamental aspect of existence, encompassing opposing forces such as good vs. evil, light vs. dark, and positive vs. negative. Carl Jung introduced the concept of the "shadow," representing the hidden aspects of ourselves that we suppress or deny.

The shadow comprises the parts of ourselves that we deem as weak, undesirable, or uncomfortable. By avoiding acknowledgment of these aspects, we inadvertently give them power, leading to internal conflict and external difficulties.

Facing the Shadow and engaging in shadow work involves confronting and acknowledging the hidden aspects of ourselves, including past traumas, negative behaviors, and uncomfortable emotions.

Through self-reflection and introspection, we take ownership of our past actions, triumphs, and wrongdoings. This process allows for healing from past traumas and the establishment of healthy boundaries for ourselves and others.

Integration and Healing
The goal of shadow work is not to eradicate the shadow but to integrate it into our lives consciously. By embracing our shadow, we gain a deeper awareness of our behaviors, perceptions, and interactions with others.

Integration enables us to regulate our moods and emotions more effectively, fostering greater stability and resilience in navigating life's challenges.

Practical Techniques for Shadow Work
Mindfulness activities, prayer, meditation, and positive affirmations serve as effective tools for shadow work. These practices help quiet the mind, connect with positive thoughts, and reinforce empowering beliefs.

For example, replacing negative thoughts such as "I am not worthy"

with positive affirmations like "I am worthy" can reshape our conscious thoughts and beliefs. Repetition and visualization of these affirmations reinforce their presence in our conscious awareness.

Seeking Support When Needed

Self-discovery and confronting the shadow can be daunting and challenging. Despite effective methods, some individuals may still struggle.

It's important to recognize when additional support is needed.

Therapists or spiritual life coaches can provide guidance, encouragement, and perspective to navigate through difficult aspects of shadow work.

Chapter guidance: Embracing shadow work is a courageous and

transformative journey toward self-awareness, healing, and personal growth. By confronting our shadow with compassion and mindfulness, we integrate all aspects of ourselves, leading to greater authenticity, resilience, and inner peace. Remember, you are not alone on this journey, and seeking support when needed is a sign of strength and self-awareness.

my journal

UNDERSTANDING FEAR IN SPIRITUALITY (Q&A)

CHAPTER 6
UNDERSTANDING FEAR IN SPIRITUALITY (Q&A)

Fear is a powerful force that can influence our thoughts, behaviors, and experiences, particularly in the realm of spirituality.

Let's delve into some common questions and insights regarding fear and its impact on spiritual growth:

Q: What are some fears you have?
Each individual may have unique fears that arise on their spiritual journey. Common fears may include fear of the unknown, fear of failure, fear of judgment, or fear of spiritual attacks.

Q: What caused you to be fearful?
Fear can stem from various sources, such as past traumas, societal conditioning, religious teachings, or personal insecurities. Additionally, encountering unfamiliar spiritual experiences or facing the prospect of exploring deeper aspects of oneself can trigger fear.

Q: How has fear hindered your life and experience?
Fear can act as a barrier to personal growth and spiritual exploration. It may lead to avoidance of certain practices or experiences, limiting one's potential for self-discovery and transformation. Fear can also manifest as anxiety, stress, or paralysis, hindering one's ability to fully engage with life and spirituality.

Q: Do you want to remain fearful?
Recognizing and acknowledging fear is the first step toward overcoming it. While fear may serve as a protective mechanism, it can also prevent us from fully embracing life's opportunities and experiences. By confronting and addressing our fears, we can cultivate courage, resilience, and a deeper sense of empowerment.

Q: Why is spirituality feared?
Spirituality is often feared due to its focus on the mysterious and unexplained aspects of existence. Spiritual experiences may involve intuitive knowing, feelings, or perceptions that transcend physical reality, which can be unsettling for some individuals. Additionally, spirituality has been demonized by certain religious teachings, leading to fear and mistrust of spiritual practices.

Q: Is sleep paralysis different from astral travel?
Sleep analysis and astral travel are distinct experiences. Sleep paralysis is often associated with a feeling of being physically immobilised while experiencing vivid dreams or hallucinations. Sleep paralysis is tied to spiritual attacks and is often accompanied by fear. In contrast, astral travel involves a conscious and controlled departure of the soul from the physical body, allowing for the exploration of spiritual realms and interactions with entities. While both experiences may involve vivid dreams, they differ in terms of control and intention.

Q: Why do people avoid acknowledging their gifts and abilities?
Many individuals may avoid acknowledging their gifts and abilities due to a lack of understanding, fear of judgment, or uncertainty about how to develop and integrate these gifts into their lives. In the early stages of spiritual development, these experiences may be unfamiliar or perceived as threatening, leading to avoidance or suppression.

Chapter Guidance: By addressing these questions and understanding the role of fear in spirituality, individuals can cultivate greater self-awareness, courage, and resilience on their spiritual journey.

Remember, fear is not an obstacle to be avoided but a challenge to be embraced and overcome in pursuit of growth and enlightenment. Fear can significantly limit our ability to tap into and utilize our spiritual gifts effectively.

Let's explore how fear manifests in various scenarios and hinders the expression of these gifts. Remember **F.E.A.R.** is an acronym for False Evidence Appearing Real. There's no true threat of immediate physical danger, no threat of a loss.

"

F.E.A.R. is an acronym for False Evidence Appearing Real. There's no true threat of immediate physical danger, no threat of a loss.

Dreams and Premonitions
Fear of dreams or premonitions coming true can lead to anxiety and avoidance of sleep, depriving individuals of restorative rest and potentially valuable insights from their dreams.

Hearing Spirits
Fear of hearing spirits or receiving messages from the spiritual realm can cause individuals to shut down their intuitive abilities, blocking communication and guidance from spiritual entities.

Communicating with the Deceased
The concept of communicating with the deceased may evoke fear and disbelief, preventing individuals from embracing opportunities for closure, healing, or spiritual connection with departed loved ones.

Spiritual Visitation
Fear of encountering spiritual entities, whether pleasant or unpleasant, can inhibit individuals from fully engaging with spiritual visitations and understanding their significance or purpose.

Healing Gifts
Fear of the unknown or uncertainty about the source of healing knowledge may discourage individuals from embracing their innate healing abilities, leading to missed opportunities for self-healing and helping others.

Clairvoyance and Message Giving
Fear of delivering messages through clairvoyance or intuitive insights can result in suppression of these abilities, causing physical discomfort and internal conflict when messages go unheeded or ignored.

Messages through Possession
Fear of spiritual possession and loss of control over one's actions or words can create barriers to channeling spiritual messages or allowing spiritual entities to communicate through individuals.

Chapter Guidance: Part 2: In each of these scenarios, fear acts as a barrier that obstructs the flow of spiritual energy and inhibits the expression of innate gifts and abilities.

By addressing and overcoming fear through self-awareness, acceptance, and spiritual practice, individuals can unlock their full potential and harness their gifts for the highest good. It is essential to cultivate trust in oneself, the divine, and the spiritual guidance that is available, allowing fear to dissipate and making way for profound spiritual growth and transformation.

CHAPTER QUESTION
What are some aspects of spirituality that you are uncomfortable with and why?

my journal

UNDERSTANDING SPIRITUAL HYGIENE

CHAPTER 7
UNDERSTANDING SPIRITUAL HYGIENE

Spiritual hygiene is paramount for maintaining well-being and balance in all aspects of our lives. Just as we prioritize physical hygiene to prevent illness and maintain health, spiritual hygiene involves practices and boundaries that safeguard our spiritual and emotional well-being.

Here's why spiritual hygiene is crucial and how it impacts various aspects of our lives:

Definition of Spiritual Hygiene
Spiritual hygiene encompasses conditions and practices that promote spiritual health and prevent negative influences from affecting our well-being. It involves setting boundaries to protect our personal space, energy, emotions, relationships, and spiritual connections.

Importance of Spiritual Hygiene
Spiritual hygiene is essential for maintaining clarity, balance, and inner peace in our lives. By cultivating healthy boundaries and practices, we safeguard ourselves against spiritual and emotional turmoil, promoting overall well-being.

Maintaining Personal Space and Energy
Setting boundaries for our personal space and energy is vital for protecting ourselves from negative influences and maintaining our energetic integrity. This includes practicing mindfulness, meditation, and energetic protection techniques to cleanse and strengthen our aura.

Emotional Well-being
Spiritual hygiene extends to our emotional health, including maintaining a baseline level of peace and harmony within ourselves. By practicing self-care, emotional awareness, and healthy coping mechanisms, we foster resilience and emotional balance.

Physical Surroundings
Our physical environment reflects our internal state and spiritual well-being. Keeping our surroundings clean, organized, and clutter-free is essential for promoting a sense of calm, clarity, and order in our lives.

Spiritual Life and Practices
Our spiritual practices and connections are central to spiritual hygiene. Engaging in regular prayer, meditation, spiritual rituals, and connecting with our spiritual community helps cleanse and recharge our spiritual energy, fostering spiritual growth and alignment with our higher purpose.

Alignment with Divine Order
Living in alignment with divine order and harmony is central to spiritual hygiene. Chaos, disorder, and negativity disrupt our connection with the divine and impede our spiritual growth. By cultivating order, peace, and positivity in our lives, we create space for divine guidance and blessings to flow freely.

Maintaining Boundaries with Personal Space
Know yourself and your comfort levels, and set clear limits on behaviors or interactions that make you uncomfortable, such as possession or unwanted intrusions.

Utilize tools such as crystals or Florida Water to protect your personal and energetically shield yourself from negative influences.

Communicate your boundaries to others, both verbally and energetically, to assertively maintain your personal space and integrity.

Protecting Your Surroundings
Avoid clutter and maintain physical cleanliness in your surroundings to allow energy to flow freely and promote a sense of calm and balance.
Use fragrances such as lavender, sweet grass, palo santo, or incense to clear and purify your space, amplifying positive energies and dispelling negativity.

Cleansing a Space
To cleanse a space, eliminate fear, and approach the process with confidence and authority. If uncomfortable, seek assistance from someone experienced in spiritual cleansing. Use various tools such as music, prayer, incense, crystals, or symbols to cleanse the space and remove negative energies. Choose music that uplifts and raises your vibrations, such as drumming, nature sounds, chanting, or music that brings you joy and positivity.

Saging and Smudging
Saging or smudging is a powerful method of cleansing a space. Light the sage until smoking Open windows and doors to allow for energy or entities to exit and enter through and move through the space from top to bottom, back to the front, don't forget corners and closets.

These steps are very important including praying, chanting, or music to remove lower-level energies. Follow up with sweet fragrances to invite positive energy and balance into the space. Repeat this process regularly.

Alternative Cleansing Methods
Wiping down surfaces or cleaning with spiritual solutions such as Florida Water, natural spring water, natural salts, or ammonia can also effectively clear and purify a space. Sweeping and mopping are spiritual practices that physically and energetically remove dirt and debris, promoting cleanliness and energetic balance.

Bathing and Spiritual Cleansing
Bathing plays a crucial role in spiritual hygiene, helping to remove negative energies and restore balance to the body and spirit.
Bathe daily for physical hygiene, visualizing negative energies being washed away. Spiritual baths can be done on occasion for specific intentions, using ingredients tailored to your goals for cleansing and attracting positivity.

Chapter Guidance: By maintaining boundaries with personal space and consistently cleansing our surroundings, we create a harmonious environment that supports our spiritual well- being and growth. Incorporating these practices into our
daily lives fosters clarity, balance, and positivity, enhancing our connection with ourselves and the divine.

CHAPTER QUESTION
What hygiene practices will you put in place?

my journal

HONORING YOUR ANCESTORS

CHAPTER 8
HONORING YOUR ANCESTORS

Honoring your ancestors is a deeply rooted practice found in many cultures around the world. It involves religious beliefs and rituals aimed at paying respects to the spirits of deceased relatives and ancestors.

Here's an exploration of the significance and practices involved in honoring ancestors. Honoring one's ancestors is a sacred practice of cultures and traditions, providing a spiritual connection to past generations and influencing the lives of future descendants.

Here's a closer look at the significance and practices involved in ancestral reverence:

Understanding Ancestral Honoring
Ancestral honoring is a sacred tradition that acknowledges the enduring presence and influence of deceased relatives and ancestors. It is based on the belief that the spirits of ancestors continue to exist beyond death and can interact with the living world.

Practices and Rituals
Ancestral altars are commonly used in ancestral honoring rituals, serving as focal points for prayers, offerings, and remembrance. These altars may be adorned with photographs, mementos, and symbolic items representing the ancestors.
Prayers, offerings, and rituals are performed as acts of reverence and gratitude towards the ancestors. Offerings may include food, drink, incense, flowers, or other items believed to be pleasing to the spirits.
Through prayers and offerings, individuals seek the guidance, blessings, and protection of their ancestors. Ancestors are viewed as mediators between the living and the divine, capable of interceding on behalf of their descendants.

Connection to Lineage
Ancestral honoring extends beyond immediate family members to encompass all ancestors within one's lineage, regardless of how far back they may be. This connection to lineage fosters a sense of continuity, identity, and belonging within the family and community.

Spiritual Guidance and Support
It is believed that ancestors can offer spiritual guidance, wisdom, and support to their living descendants. By honoring and maintaining a connection with their ancestors, individuals seek to benefit from their ancestral blessings and wisdom in navigating life's challenges and decisions.

Cultural Significance:
Ancestral honoring practices vary across cultures and traditions, reflecting unique beliefs, customs, and rituals specific to each community. Despite these variations, the underlying reverence for ancestors and the importance of familial ties remain central themes.

Continuing the Tradition
Honoring ancestors is a timeless tradition passed down through generations, preserving the spiritual connection between past, present, and future. By continuing these rituals, individuals uphold their cultural heritage and honor the contributions and sacrifices of their ancestors.

Influencing Future Generations
Ancestral reverence is believed to bless and watch over later generations, offering spiritual guidance, protection, and blessings to their living loved ones. Prayers, offerings, and gifts are made to appease and gain favor with the ancestors, ensuring their continued blessings upon the family.

Ensuring the Souls Remain in the Light:
After a loved one transitions from the physical world, it is important to pray for their soul's journey and make offerings to keep them in the light. This ensures that their spirit cannot be used in negative ways and helps maintain the purity of their soul in the afterlife.

Ongoing Honoring Practices
While repasses are common in many cultures as a way to honor deceased loved ones, ancestral reverence should be an ongoing practice. Regular prayers, offerings, and remembrance keep the memories and souls of the ancestors alive and in a positive light.

Creating Sacred Space:
Ancestral altars provide a private and personal space for honoring and connecting with the ancestors. These altars should be separate from high-traffic areas and maintained with cleanliness and tidiness. Keeping the altar fresh and beautiful reflects the reverence and respect for the ancestors.

Biblical References:
Biblical passages, such as Deuteronomy 4:37, acknowledge the importance of honoring the prayers of ancestors and teaching future generations about their legacy. This reinforces the significance of ancestral reverence in religious and spiritual contexts.

Altar Considerations:
Not everyone needs to have an ancestral altar, as altars are requested by the Spirit. Other ways to honor loved ones include cooking their favorite foods, playing their favorite music, and speaking positively of their memory.

Elements of an Ancestral Altar:
An ancestral altar should represent the connection to the ancestor and may include elements such as candles for light, flowers, cooked food, or any items that hold significance to the intended purpose of the altar.

OTHER TYPES OF ALTARS
In addition to ancestral altars, other types of altars may serve specific purposes such as protection, prosperity, or spiritual connection. These altars are used to pray for specific intentions and manifest desires in alignment with spiritual principles.

Chapter Guidance: the practice of ancestral reverence is a profound expression of gratitude, respect, and connection to past generations.

Through prayers, offerings, and remembrance, individuals honor the legacy of their ancestors and maintain a spiritual bond that transcends time, space, and death. Maintaining a code of ethics in our interactions with ancestors and spirit guides is vital for nurturing a harmonious and respectful relationship within the spiritual realm.

This includes creating a sacred space for our ancestors to visit voluntarily, as summoning spirits can bring serious risks and repercussions. It's crucial to honor their agency and autonomy in choosing when and how they connect with us. Seeking consent before communication and expressing gratitude and reverence for their guidance and presence are essential aspects of this ethical framework.

These practices uphold integrity, respect, and mindfulness, ensuring that our spiritual interactions are conducted with care and responsibility.

my journal

MANIFESTATION

CHAPTER 9
MANIFESTATION

Manifestation typically refers to the process of bringing something into existence or reality through the power of intention, belief, and focused energy. It's often associated with practices like visualization, positive thinking, and goal-setting, with the belief that one can attract desired outcomes into their life by aligning their thoughts and actions with their goals.

Manifestation Practices: Techniques and rituals aimed at bringing desired outcomes into reality through focused intention, visualization, and belief. These practices can
include affirmations, visualization exercises, meditation, gratitude journaling, vision boards, and various forms of energy work.

They are based on the principle that our thoughts and emotions have the power to shape our reality, and by aligning our thoughts and emotions with our goals, we can attract what we desire into our lives.

Chapter Questions

What goals or dreams have you always wanted to accomplish?

How long have you had this goals or dreams?

What steps have you made to accomplish your goals or dreams?

Notes:

Chapter Guidance: When attempting to manifest something into reality, using your imagination paired with positive intentions, effective planning and preparation is considered the purest form of magic.

7 THINGS ABOUT THE LAW OF ATTRACTION YOU NEED TO KNOW

Made famous by the book "The Secret" — the law of attraction is a physical law which put simply is attracting into our lives whatever we put attention, energy and focus on for good and for bad. In this infographic we will list 7 things you need to know about putting the law of attraction into action for your life

1. FOCUS ON WHAT YOU WANT

Foucusing on what you want is the contrary of focusing on what is. Put your emphasis and energy on the things you want to manifest in your life

2. VISUALIZATION IMPROVES PHYSICAL PERFORMANCE

As many champion athletes will attest spending time on creative visualization directly influences yout physical abilities

3. IT WILL TRANSFORM YOUR BELIEFS ABOUT SUCCESS

Once you adopt a core belief in the law of attraction.You can see that success is a commodity that is available to everyone

4. GOOD VIBRATIONS

What you give is what you get there are only two kinds of vibes : positive and negative ... make sureyou give out good vibrations to get good vibrations back

5. ALLOWANCE

Allowance is the absence of a negative vibration and is a state where resistance doesn't exist. You fully allow yourself to reach a goal only when you remove the doubts you have

6. TRUST YOUR INSTINCTS

Proponents of the law of attraction argue that you should believe in the accuracy of your own intuition, letting your emotions naturally draw you towards the right path

7. GRATITUDE IS A MAGNET FOR GOOD

Gratitude is to feel thankful for the things you already have. When you do that, you will attract more and more of the things you are thankful for

CHAPTER 10 TOOLS & TOKENS

Spiritual tools and tokens can vary greatly depending on one's beliefs and practices. The effectiveness of these tools often lies in the intention, belief or energy of the practitioner.

Some common examples include

1. **Crystals:** Believed to have various energies and properties that can aid in meditation, healing, and manifestation.

2. **Tarot or Oracle cards:** Used for divination and gaining insight into one's life and circumstances.

3. **Incense and Sage**: Burned to cleanse energy, purify spaces, and enhance spiritual practices.

4. **Meditation Cushions or Altars:** Creating a dedicated space for meditation and spiritual reflection.

5. **Prayer Beads or Malas:** Used for counting prayers, mantras, or affirmations during meditation.

6. **Essential Oils:** Utilized for aromatherapy and enhancing spiritual and physical experiences.

7. **Symbols and Talismans**: Objects imbued with specific meanings or energies, such as religious symbols or personal amulets.

8. **Ritual Tools:** Such as wands, athames, or candles, are used in ceremonial magic or rituals.

CANDLES

What does a candle represent?
A candle serves as a physical representation of oneself or something one wishes to attract or remove in spiritual practice.

How do you use candles in spirituality?
Candles are utilized in various ways in spiritual work. After selecting a candle's color and size, it is dressed with herbs, oils, crystals, prayers, and other ingredients depending on the specific intention of the work being done.

What does the color of a candle represent?
Red: Represents passion, potency, stamina, fresh starts, good luck, confidence, willpower, physical strength, courage, and determination. Associated with the Root Chakra..

Orange: Enhances quick action, mental activities, luck in career, networking, and legal affairs. Associated with the Sacral Chakra.

Yellow: Enhances joy, happiness, learning, mental clarity, confidence, wisdom, logical thinking. Associated with the Solar Plexus Chakra.

Green: Attracts abundance, success, prosperity, health, harmony, and growth. Associated with the Heart Chakra.
Blue: Enhances focus, memory, justice, inspiration, peace of mind, truth, healing, and connection with the higher self. Associated with the Throat Chakra.

Purple/Indigo: Enhances wisdom, meditation, divination, spiritual awareness, uncovering secrets, and knowledge. Associated with the Third Eye and Crown Chakras.

Black: Used for protection, banishing negative energy, reversing curses, unblocking stagnant energy, stopping bad habits, and ending unhealthy situations.
White: Represents protection, new beginnings, purity, healing, truth, meditation, peace, gratitude, and harmony. It can be used in place of any other color.

Blue: Enhances focus, memory, justice, inspiration, peace of mind, truth, healing, and connection with the higher self. Associated with the Throat Chakra.

Purple/Indigo: Enhances wisdom, meditation, divination, spiritual awareness, uncovering secrets, and knowledge. Associated with the Third Eye and Crown Chakras.

Black: Used for protection, banishing negative energy, reversing curses, unblocking stagnant energy, stopping bad habits, and ending unhealthy situations.

White: Represents protection, new beginnings, purity, healing, truth, meditation, peace, gratitude, and harmony. It can be used in place of any other color.

Brown: Grounding, neutrality, understanding, balance, trust, connection with animal guides.

Pink: Enhances happiness, harmony, empathy, intimacy, strengthening relationships, facilitating healing, reconciliation, forgiveness, emotional healing.

Multicolored: Used for connecting with ancestors, and as an all-purpose candle.

Dressing Candles:

Why would you dress a candle?
Dressing a candle involves anointing it with oils, herbs, or other materials to enhance its energy and align it with the specific intention for which it is being used. This process amplifies the candle's purpose, making it more effective in spiritual work.

Chapter Guidance: Understanding the symbolism and associations of candle colors allows practitioners to select the appropriate candles for their specific intentions in spiritual work, facilitating the manifestation of desired outcomes.

HERBS AND OILS USED IN SPIRITUALITY

What herbs do you use in spirituality?
Practitioners use a wide variety of herbs in spirituality, often guided by intuition and personal preference.

What do herbs represent?
Herbs symbolize life, love, healing, cleansing, purity, strength, and vitality. They are seen as potent tools for enhancing spiritual practices and rituals.

COMMON HERBS USED IN SPIRITUALITY AND THEIR PURPOSE

Sage: Used for spiritual cleansing of people or spaces, promoting healing, clarity, wisdom, and peace.

Rosemary: Enhances clarity of the mind, strengthens the connection to ancestors, and wards off negative energy.

Thyme: Enhances psychic powers, and promotes good health, wealth, prophetic dreams, and visions.

Bay Leaf: Attracts wealth, prosperity, and love, and promotes stress relief, relaxation, lucid dreams, clairvoyance, and astral travel.

Basil: Reduces negative energy, brings harmony to the elements, purifies spaces, promotes stress relief, relaxation, and the manifestation of love.

Vervain: Protects against evil spells, and negative energy, and purifies sacred places, such as altars, ceremonial implements, temples, and private dwellings.

Each herb carries its unique energy and properties, making them valuable assets in spiritual practices and rituals.

OILS

Why are oils used in spirituality?
Oils are used in spirituality for their potent energy and properties, often derived from herbs and flowers.

What are they used for?
They are used for dressing candles, creating tonics, and baths, infusing other tokens, and enhancing the energy needed for manifestation.

When do you use the oils?
Oils are used as needed in spiritual practices, often in place of or in conjunction with herbs or flowers.

CRYSTALS

What are crystals?
Crystals are natural formations of minerals with unique energetic properties that are used in various spiritual practices.

Common Crystals and Their Uses:
Common crystals include quartz, amethyst, citrine, rose quartz, and others, each with its unique properties used for healing, protection, manifestation, and spiritual growth.

Psalms: In spiritual and religious practices, particularly within Christianity and Judaism, various Psalms are commonly used for meditation, prayer, and spiritual guidance.

Here are a few examples of some commonly used psalms:

1. **Psalm 23:** Known as the Shepherd's Psalm, it provides comfort and assurance, emphasizing God's care and protection.

2. **Psalm 27:** Focuses on trust and confidence in God, even in times of fear and uncertainty.

3. **Psalm 51:** A prayer for forgiveness and cleansing, often used during repentance and seeking spiritual renewal.

4. **Psalm 91**: Known as the Psalm of Protection, it emphasizes God's refuge and shelter during times of trouble.

5. **Psalm 121**: A Psalm of assurance, emphasizing God's constant presence and help in times of need.

6. **Psalm 139:** Celebrates God's omniscience and omnipresence, affirming the individual's unique identity and purpose.

These Psalms, among others, are often recited, meditated upon, or incorporated into spiritual rituals to foster a deeper connection with the divine, seek guidance, or find solace in times of difficulty.

How will you use the Psalms in your spiritual practice?

Note: Psalms are often referred to as "The First Book of Spells" and are used in spirituality for their poetic and powerful
words, recited or prayed to invoke specific intentions, blessings, protection, and guidance.

Prayer and Intention in Spirituality:
Prayer and intention are essential components of spirituality, used to connect with divine energies, set intentions, express gratitude, seek guidance, and manifest desires.

What is fasting and prayer?
Fasting and prayer are spiritual practices found in many religious and spiritual traditions in which individuals abstain from food or certain activities for some time while devoting themselves to prayer, meditation, and spiritual reflection.

Tarot Cards

What is tarot?
The tarot is a deck of cards typically consisting of 78 cards divided into the Major Arcana and Minor Arcana. Each card is rich in symbolism and imagery, representing different archetypes, themes, and aspects of life.

How is it used in spirituality?
Tarot cards are used in spirituality for divination, self-reflection, guidance, and insight into various aspects of life, including relationships, career, personal growth, and spiritual development.

Why is it used?
Tarot cards are used to gain insight, clarity, and understanding about present circumstances, as well as to explore potential future outcomes. They can also be used for introspection and personal growth.

When is it used?
Tarot cards can be used at any time when seeking guidance, clarity, or insight into a situation or aspect of life. They are often used during spiritual practices, rituals, or when facing important decisions or challenges

Chapter Guidance: The accuracy of spiritual messages conveyed through tarot cards often depends on the integrity and authenticity of the reader.

Unfortunately, not all tarot readers possess intuitive accuracy, as the efficacy of their readings relies heavily on spiritual guidance. Additionally, the presence of fraudulent individuals in the
industry can exploit vulnerabilities for financial gain. It's crucial for individuals to approach tarot readings with discernment and to engage in self-reflection, as interpretations can vary based on perspective and circumstances.

my journal

UNDERSTANDING CHAKRAS

CHAPTER 11
UNDERSTANDING CHAKRAS

How many chakras are there?
According to some spiritual traditions, there are said to be 112 chakras in the body, arranged into seven dimensions with sixteen aspects in each dimension. These dimensions form the basis for the seven chakras commonly referenced in practices such as
Yoga.

The Seven Commonly Referred Chakras
Crown Chakra
Throat Chakra
Third Eye Chakra
Heart Chakra
Solar Plexus Chakra
Sacral Chakra
Root Chakra

What Each Chakra Represents
 Root Chakra (Muladhara): Located at the base of the spine, the root chakra represents our foundation, stability, and sense of security.

 Sacral Chakra (Swadhisthana): Positioned in the lower
abdomen, the sacral chakra governs our emotions, creativity, and sexual energy.

 Solar Plexus Chakra (Manipura): Situated in the upper
abdomen, the solar plexus chakra is associated with our self-esteem, confidence, and personal power.

 Heart Chakra (Anahata): Found in the center of the chest, the heart chakra governs love, compassion, and relationships.

 Throat Chakra (Vishuddha): Located in the throat area, the throat chakra represents communication, self-expression, and truth..

Third Eye Chakra (Ajna): Positioned between the eyebrows, the third eye chakra is associated with intuition, insight, and spiritual awareness.

Crown Chakra (Sahasrara): Located at the top of the head, the crown chakra represents our connection to spirituality, divine
wisdom, and higher consciousness

Chakra affirmations are positive statements that are used to balance, align, and activate the energy centers in the body and mind.

Here are some affirmation examples for each of the seven main chakras:
1. Root Chakra (Muladhara):
"I am - grounded, stable, and secure. I trust in the abundance of the universe."

2. Sacral Chakra (Swadhisthana): "I feel - embrace pleasure and abundance. My emotions flow freely, and I nurture my creative
energy."

3. Solar Plexus Chakra (Manipura): "I do - speak confidence and empowerment. I trust my inner wisdom and make decisions with courage."

4. Heart Chakra (Anahata): "I love - I radiate love. I forgive myself and others, and I open my heart to compassion."

5. Throat Chakra (Vishuddha): "I speak - I express myself clearly and authentically. My voice is powerful, and I speak my truth with
integrity."

6. Third Eye Chakra (Ajna): "I see - my intuition, and I see the truth in all situations. My mind is open to new insights and wisdom."

7. Crown Chakra (Sahasrara): "I know - I am connected to the
divine. I am one with the universe, and I am guided by higher consciousness."

Repeat these affirmations regularly while focusing on each chakra to promote balance, healing, and alignment of your energy centers.

Chapter Guidance: Understanding and balancing these chakras is believed to promote overall health, well-being, and spiritual growth. Practices such as meditation, yoga, and energy healing techniques are often used to align and harmonize the chakras, promoting a sense of balance and vitality in mind, body, and spirit.

CHAPTER QUESTION
What practices, techniques, and affirmations will you incorporate in efforts to balance your Chakras?

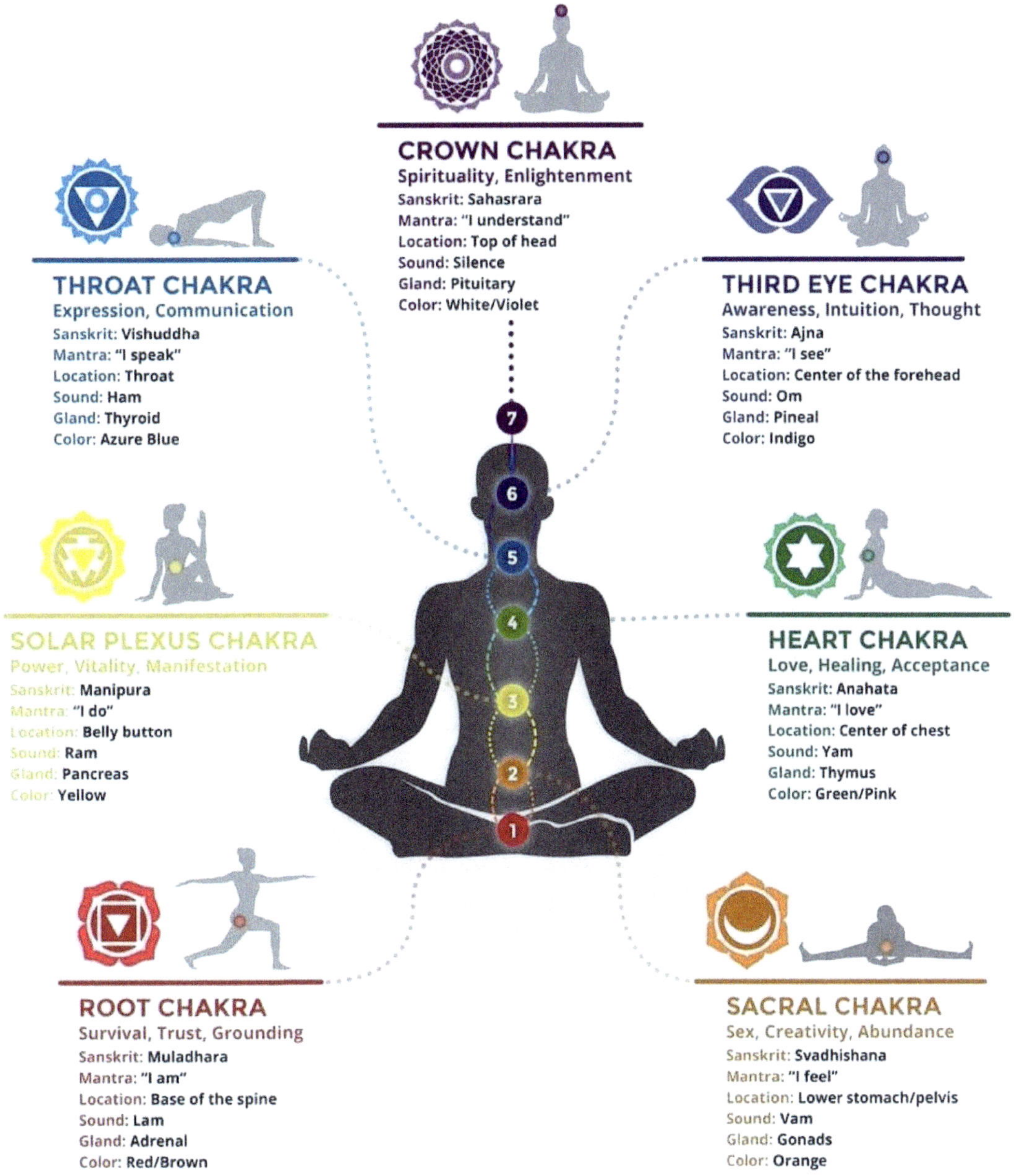

CROWN CHAKRA
Spirituality, Enlightenment
Sanskrit: **Sahasrara**
Mantra: "I understand"
Location: **Top of head**
Sound: **Silence**
Gland: **Pituitary**
Color: **White/Violet**

THIRD EYE CHAKRA
Awareness, Intuition, Thought
Sanskrit: **Ajna**
Mantra: "I see"
Location: **Center of the forehead**
Sound: **Om**
Gland: **Pineal**
Color: **Indigo**

THROAT CHAKRA
Expression, Communication
Sanskrit: **Vishuddha**
Mantra: "I speak"
Location: **Throat**
Sound: **Ham**
Gland: **Thyroid**
Color: **Azure Blue**

HEART CHAKRA
Love, Healing, Acceptance
Sanskrit: **Anahata**
Mantra: "I love"
Location: **Center of chest**
Sound: **Yam**
Gland: **Thymus**
Color: **Green/Pink**

SOLAR PLEXUS CHAKRA
Power, Vitality, Manifestation
Sanskrit: **Manipura**
Mantra: "I do"
Location: **Belly button**
Sound: **Ram**
Gland: **Pancreas**
Color: **Yellow**

SACRAL CHAKRA
Sex, Creativity, Abundance
Sanskrit: **Svadhishana**
Mantra: "I feel"
Location: **Lower stomach/pelvis**
Sound: **Vam**
Gland: **Gonads**
Color: **Orange**

ROOT CHAKRA
Survival, Trust, Grounding
Sanskrit: **Muladhara**
Mantra: "I am"
Location: **Base of the spine**
Sound: **Lam**
Gland: **Adrenal**
Color: **Red/Brown**

my journal

CALENDAR CYCLES

CHAPTER 12
CALENDAR CYCLES

In many spiritual traditions, days, months, numbers, and even colors are believed to carry energetic vibrations that can influence intentions and enhance spiritual practices.

Here's a brief overview:

1. Days: Each day of the week is associated with different planetary energies and attributes, which can affect mood, productivity, and spiritual practices. For example, Sunday is often associated with the sun and is considered a day of renewal and spiritual growth.

2. Months: Similarly, each month is associated with specific energetic qualities and themes. For example, January is often seen as a month of new beginnings and fresh starts, while October might be associated with transformation and introspection.

3. Colors: Colors are believed to have unique energetic vibrations that can influence emotions, thoughts, and intentions. For example, red is often associated with passion and vitality, while blue is linked to calmness and communication.

4. Numbers: In numerology and other spiritual practices, numbers are believed to carry symbolic meanings and energetic vibrations. For example, the number 7 is often associated with spirituality, intuition, and inner wisdom.

By incorporating these elements into spiritual practices, individuals may enhance their intentions, align with specific energies, and deepen their spiritual experiences. However, interpretations can vary widely depending on cultural beliefs and personal experiences.

The spiritual meanings associated with each day of the week vary depending on different cultures, beliefs, and traditions.

Here's a general overview:

1. Sunday: Often associated with renewal, reflection, and spiritual growth. In many cultures, Sunday is considered a day for rest and worship.

2. Monday: Symbolizes new beginnings, intuition, and emotions. It's a good day for setting intentions and focusing on personal growth.

3. Tuesday: Often linked to energy, action, and courage. It's a day for making bold decisions and taking proactive steps towards goals.

4. Wednesday: Associated with communication, wisdom, and mental clarity. It's a good day for learning, teaching, and seeking guidance.

5. Thursday: Symbolizes expansion, abundance, and prosperity. It's a day for gratitude, generosity, and attracting positive opportunities.

6. Friday: Linked to love, relationships, and creativity. It's a day for expressing affection, enjoying the arts, and nurturing connections.

7. Saturday: Often associated with grounding, discipline, and introspection. It's a good day for planning, organizing, and reflecting on achievements.

my journal

ELEMENTAL ENERGY

CHAPTER 13
ELEMENTAL ENERGY

What is elemental energy?

The elements refer to the fundamental building blocks of the natural world, including earth, water, fire, air, and sometimes spirit. Elemental energy is the energy associated with each element, believed to influence different aspects of life and spirituality.

The Sun and the Moon are both very important and powerful elemental tools in spirituality. They are the oldest elements, they were and still are vital to our existence.

Sun:

How do you work with the sun in spirituality?

Working with the sun in spirituality involves harnessing its energy for various purposes such as purification, healing, vitality, growth, and enlightenment. Practices may include sun salutations, meditation during sunrise or sunset, or rituals honoring solar energy.

THE MOON

Moon Phases: many people believe that the phases of the moon can have spiritual significance and influence energy. Practices like setting intentions or charging crystals during specific lunar phases are common in various spiritual traditions.

The belief is that aligning with the moon's energy can enhance manifestation efforts and the effectiveness of spiritual tools and tokens.

New Moon: New beginnings, planning, and preparation.
Waxing Crescent: Set intentions, and plant seeds.
First Quarter: Forward movement takes action.
Waxing Gibbous: Meditate, align, and refocus.
Full Moon: Manifest this is the time of harvest and creativity.
Waning Gibbous: gratitude, acts of service.
Last Quarter: Release a time for shadow work and self-reflection.

What is a Mercury retrograde?
Mercury retrograde is an astrological phenomenon that occurs when the planet Mercury appears to move backward in its orbit from our perspective on Earth. It is an optical illusion caused by the relative positions of Mercury and Earth as they orbit the Sun.

What does it represent?
In astrology, Mercury retrograde is often associated with communication issues, misunderstandings, delays, and disruptions in various areas such as travel, finance, and technology. This period is known for its potential for confusion and chaos, as things may not unfold as expected.

What are some of the principles to understand what happens during Mercury retrograde?
Some principles to understand during Mercury retrograde include:
Increased likelihood of miscommunications and misunderstandings
Delays and disruptions in travel and technology
Revisiting past issues or unfinished business
Heightened introspection and reflection

What are some of the guidelines followed during Mercury retrograde and why?
Some guidelines to follow during Mercury retrograde include:
Double-checking communications and agreements for clarity
Avoiding making major decisions or signing contracts if possible
Backing up important data and being prepared for technology glitches allowing extra time for travel and being flexible with plans

my journal

CAREFUL CONSUMPTION

CHAPTER 14
CAREFUL CONSUMPTION

In spirituality, the concept of careful consumption extends beyond just what we eat or drink. It encompasses all aspects of our lives, including spiritual, physical, mental, emotional, and financial consumption.

Here's a breakdown:

Spiritual Consumption:
Be mindful of the spiritual content you consume, such as books, teachings, and media. Ensure that they align with your beliefs and values and contribute positively to your spiritual growth.

Physical Consumption:
Watch what you eat and drink, opting for nourishing foods that support your physical health and well-being. Similarly, be mindful of the substances you put into your body, avoiding harmful or addictive substances.

Consider the media you consume visually, such as TV shows, movies, and social media content. Choose content that uplifts and inspires you, rather than promoting negative emotions or values.

Mental Consumption:
Be aware of the information you expose yourself to, including news, articles, and conversations. Filter out negativity and focus on knowledge and ideas that enrich your mental faculties and promote growth.

Engage in activities that stimulate your mind, such as reading, learning new skills, or engaging in creative endeavors.

Emotional Consumption:
Pay attention to the emotions you allow yourself to feel and express. Surround yourself with people who uplift and support you emotionally, and set boundaries with those who drain your energy or promote negativity.

Practice self-care rituals that nourish your emotional well-being, such as meditation, journaling, or spending time in nature.

Financial Consumption:
Be conscious of your spending habits and financial decisions. Prioritize investments that align with your values and long-term goals, and avoid excessive or impulsive spending that may lead to financial stress.

Consider the impact of your purchases on the environment and society, opting for ethical and sustainable products whenever possible.

Consider the media you consume visually, such as TV shows, movies, and social media content. Choose content that uplifts and inspires you, rather than promoting negative emotions or values.

Mental Consumption:
Be aware of the information you expose yourself to, including news, articles, and conversations. Filter out negativity and focus on knowledge and ideas that enrich your mental faculties and promote growth.

Engage in activities that stimulate your mind, such as reading, learning new skills, or engaging in creative endeavors.

Emotional Consumption:
Pay attention to the emotions you allow yourself to feel and express. Surround yourself with people who uplift and support you emotionally, and set boundaries with those who drain your energy or promote negativity.

Practice self-care rituals that nourish your emotional well-being, such as meditation, journaling, or spending time in nature.

Financial Consumption:
Be conscious of your spending habits and financial decisions. Prioritize investments that align with your values and long-term goals, and avoid excessive or impulsive spending that may lead to financial stress.

Consider the impact of your purchases on the environment and society, opting for ethical and sustainable products whenever possible.

Chapter Guidance: By practicing careful consumption in all aspects of your life, you can cultivate a more intentional and fulfilling existence that aligns with your spiritual beliefs and aspirations.

my journal

my journal

my journal

my journal

my journal

my journal

THANK YOU

In closing It's been a pleasure assisting you on your journey of self-discovery and spiritual exploration. Wishing you continued growth, clarity, and fulfillment on your path.

S P I R I T U A L E S S E N T I A L S . S T O R E

References:

The Bible: For spiritual seekers and believers, the Bible serves as a source of inspiration, comfort, wisdom, and guidance. It offers insights into the nature of God, the meaning of life, human nature, morality, and salvation. Many people turn to the Bible for guidance in times of joy, sorrow, uncertainty, or seeking answers to life's big questions.

The internet: has become an increasingly valuable resource for spiritual seekers, offering a wide range of information, teachings, practices, and communities for exploration and growth. Here are some ways the internet serves as a spiritual reference. While the internet offers valuable resources it's important to approach online information with discernment and critical thinking, considering the credibility and reliability of sources. Additionally, balancing online exploration with offline practices such as meditation, nature walks, and community involvement can help maintain a holistic approach to spiritual growth and well-being

The chapter on Shadow Work:
In this chapter, where you discuss the concept of shadow work and Carl Jung's insights, you can reference the article from the Academy of Ideas titled "Carl Jung and the Shadow: The Hidden Power of Our Dark Side"

https://academyofideas.com/2015/12/carl-jung-and-the-shadow-the-hidden-power-of-our-dark-side/).

This source provides valuable insights into Jungian psychology and the importance of confronting our shadow selves.

The chapter on Seeking Help:
Working with a spiritual and life coach like Lovenda McHayle-Jack can indeed lead to a transformative journey of personal growth and self-discovery. Lovenda McHayle-Jack, with her experience, knowledge, and straightforward guidance, can provide valuable support and practical tools to help you on your journey

https://www.spiritualessentials.store/ to book a coaching session.

When discussing the importance of seeking professional help, you can reference Psychology Today (https://www.psychologytoday.com/us) as a valuable resource for finding therapy resources in the US. Psychology Today offers a comprehensive directory of therapists, psychologists, and counselors, making it a reliable source for individuals seeking mental health support.

ACKNOWLEDGMENTS

I would like to express my heartfelt gratitude to my loving family and spiritual tribe for their unwavering support and encouragement throughout the years. Your love and belief in me have been a constant source of inspiration.

Special thanks to Dr. Dilice Robertson for her invaluable assistance in getting this project off the ground and for sharing her wealth of knowledge and insights.

I am immensely grateful to Michele Thompkins & Shenika Coombs for their exceptional editorial skills and dedication to refining this project to its highest potential.

And finally, to you, the reader, thank you for joining me on this incredible journey. I have no doubt that your contributions to the spiritual community will be profound and far-reaching. Your participation has been instrumental in bringing this dream to fruition, and for that, I am truly thankful.

With deepest appreciation,
Love Jack

Printed in Great Britain
by Amazon